Out there beyond the borders are the shivering dunes, heaps
upon heaps of blinding sand all acrawl in the wind, drifting
and reforming with a faint, stridulent rustle…

–Mary Austin, from Lost Borders, *1909*

Winter storm clouds tease with the potential of rain, but leave the Grapevine Mountains parched. The 140-mile-long basin of
Death Valley is the driest area in the United States.
Opposite: The crest of Eureka Sand Dunes rises 700 feet above the desert floor.

An ephemeral lake created by a winter storm covers the floor of Panamint Valley and serenely reflects the Cottonwood Mountains.
Opposite: A young cottontop cactus (Echinocactus polycephalus) *protects itself with sharp spines.*

Death Valley

NATIONAL PARK

Photography by

FRED & RANDI HIRSCHMANN

Environmental History by Mark A. Schlenz

COMPANION PRESS
Santa Barbara, California

Companion Press
464 Terrace Road
Santa Barbara, California 93109
Jane Freeburg, Publisher/Editor
Designed by Lucy Brown

Printed in Hong Kong
through Bolton Associates,
San Rafael, California

ISBN 0-944197-51-5
First Printing

CONTENTS

*Pinyon pine cone, driftwood, and patterned
rocks on the floor of Last Chance Canyon.
Opposite: Joshua tree silhouetted at dawn,
Darwin Plateau.*

Salt pans of Devils Golf Course, with the Amargosa Range beyond.
Opposite: Last light on the Grapevine Mountains near Red Wall Canyon.

DESERT CANYON EXPLORATIONS

by Fred Hirschmann

When Randi and I visit Death Valley, we know we are going to visit rocks: rocks forming massive cliffs, rocks collecting into huge alluvial fans, billions of tiny ground-down rocks that make up the sands of Death Valley's classic dunes. Few places in North America speak so eloquently of geology in action. For here in Death Valley—and the surrounding mountains and basins—the Earth's bones are laid bare for all to explore. No green skin of vegetation hides the underlying geology, yet close to a thousand plant species eke out a living here by surviving extremes—adapting to summertime air temperatures in excess of 120°F, ground temperatures of a sizzling 190°F, and precipitation that averages less than two inches of rain annually. In such an arid environment, it pays to live far from your neighbors, to garner a spot where extensive root systems find little competition for scant and uncertain moisture. Consequently, space abounds between plants. When we look across the landscape what we see are rocks.

Our planet may be known as a watery world with eighty percent of its surface covered by oceans, lakes, and rivers. But in Death Valley, surface water is a rare commodity. When we hike in Death Valley, we feel its pervasive dryness with every breath drawn through our lungs. For a day-long hike in Death Valley two gallons of water per person may be insufficient. When J. R. Ross wrote about Death Valley in 1868 for the United States' first mineral resources survey, he reported,

> I have heard complaint that the thermometer failed to show the true heat because the mercury dried up. Everything dries; wagons dry; men dry; chickens dry; there is no juice left in anything living or dead, by the close of summer.

Yet in this place where the liquid elixir of life is so rare, water is the grand agent which has

Colorful rock formations of eroded beds of sandstone and volcanic ash near Red Pass at the head of Titus Canyon.

washes. Flash floods act as nature's conveyor belts, moving rock off the mountains through steep canyons and onto the basins where huge fans of alluvium are created. Boulders measuring 30 feet in diameter have washed ten miles southeast of Telescope Peak. Tremendous floods transported these rocks! Geologists estimate 8,000 feet of fill has been deposited in Death Valley in the vicinity of Mesquite Flat. Faulting and down-slipping allow the valley to subside faster than sediments can fill it back up. Consequently, the surface of Death Valley warps well below sea level to a low elevation of -282 feet near Badwater.

Heavy rains transport sediments—and they also occasionally create ephemeral lakes. Randi remembers:

After a heavy November rain, we drove to the Racetrack and were ecstatic to find a lake on the far side of the playa. We quickly gathered our camera gear and hiked a half-mile to the water's edge. Across the shallow lake the blue sky and golden-brown hues of Ubehebe Peak reflected serenely in the water. We lingered throughout the day, spending hours with this ephemeral lake. Early the next morning, we once again hiked across the playa and to our surprise, the lake had vanished. We pondered the water's disappearance, then remembered strong, cold winds that came up the previous evening. The lake had been blown across unflooded portions of the playa and absorbed into the ground. Ice crystals, formed between the playa's mud cracks, remained the only evidence of the lake's existence. We were reminded how fleeting desert events can be—and the importance of taking time to experience these special moments.

sculpted such stupendous scenery. Coast Ranges and the Sierra Nevada—and then the Inyo, Argus, and Panamint Ranges—wring Pacific moisture out of most eastward-traveling clouds. Winter weather systems that dump many feet of snow in the Sierra may bring only dust storms or brilliant sunsets to Death Valley. Occasionally a storm arrives from a more southerly direction and works its way up the back side of the ranges, perhaps the remnant of a rare Pacific hurricane or a winter cyclone following a storm track bent far south by a strong El Niño. Either way when rains do come to Death Valley, they can be torrential.

Death Valley lacks the soils to absorb runoff. The parched, rocky landscape serves as a huge catch basin to feed myriad gullies and

When day hiking in Death Valley, we often take long, arduous strolls up alluvial fans to their canyon mouths. The variety of rocks carpeting the fans provides hints of the wonders we will find when the canyon walls narrow. A chunk of malachite predicts that perhaps we will discover a vein of brilliant green copper ore and the abandoned workings of a long-forgotten prospector. A fossiliferous limestone pebble may announce the presence of an entire wall full of circular crinoid stems, brachiopods, and other fossils from an ancient sea. We recognize advantages to starting explorations by going uphill. We try to tackle much of the strenuous, exposed hiking during the cooler hours of morning—and accomplish our return trip in late afternoon's heat headed downhill. Also, many of Death Valley's canyons contain impassable dryfalls. When approached from below, we assess each obstruction for possible routes to scramble farther up canyon. If a dryfall cannot be circumvented, we walk back down canyon with the knowledge that we may have missed a secret wonder, but we are safe from being trapped within a canyon.

When starting canyon hikes from above, we carry a climbing rope to lower packs and cameras over the dryfalls and to rappel. Even so, there is always the danger that we will arrive at a later dryfall which proves impassable. There is something irresistible about exploring just a little bit farther, or pushing the envelope perhaps more than we should, by passing over just one more dryfall. Curiosity nags us to discover what lies ahead. But we also remember

Death Valley's rocks offer a harsh, unforgiving environment.

Ferns and cattails thrive at Darwin Falls in the Argus Range.

As Randi and I began a two-day hike through the heart of Tin Mountain down Bighorn Gorge, we remembered a similar hike taken some years before by friends Esy Fields, Virginia Rosen, and Andrea Sharon. The threesome were savvy desert travelers with many miles of Death Valley exploration ground into their hiking boots. They, like us, had a friend drive them up the long, rough four-wheel drive track around White Top Mountain to the crest of the Cottonwood Mountains in the dark of night. With golden sunrise light luring Esy, Virginia, and Andrea to start their hike early,

Water-carved limestone narrows in Bighorn Gorge. Dryfalls often occur in such narrows.

Their first attempt involved carefully climbing a series of steep, exposed ledges. Esy remembers:

When my knees started nervously knocking, we stopped. I told the others, "I can't do this." I was really unsure about the route and felt we shouldn't be up there. People fall because they keep on pushing… Our next attempt was pretty hairy. We back-tracked farther up-canyon and found a quite steep ridge. We climbed it mostly on our knees and stomachs. The slope was full of loose, rotten rocks that came out when we tried to use them for hand and footholds. We made it over the top, then carefully climbed back down to the canyon below the dryfall. We would have been much more worried had we known we were in the wrong canyon.

The trio made it over additional drop-offs. Virginia slipped and whacked her head, but was not seriously hurt. Darkness descended, but luckily they had flashlights. They finally hiked out of the Cottonwoods Mountains on an alluvial fan eight miles south of their intended exit near the Mesquite Springs Campground. Friends, already out searching, were relieved to see their flashlights twinkling against the dark face of White Top Mountain.

they ventured down a path past old mine workings and dropped into a drainage. The canyon was beautiful with highly polished walls, deep twisting narrows, a palette of colorful rock formations, and many dryfalls. At first, the dryfalls did not worry them; they had brought along a rope as they knew Bighorn Gorge had numerous drop-offs, but previous hikers reported routes could be found around them. Esy, Virginia, and Andrea's problem, unbeknownst to them, was they were *not in* Bighorn Gorge.

They slithered down some dryfalls and scrambled around others, using their rope once. Then the canyon narrowed and spilled twenty feet down a vertical chute that was undercut at the bottom. They decided this was not a dryfall they could climb back up, and ventured back up canyon looking for a way around the chasm.

When Randi and I started our own Bighorn Gorge hike, we checked, double-checked, and triple-checked that we were dropping into the proper drainage—it had been dark when we arrived the night before, and it was difficult to assess exactly where we were. The top of the Cottonwood Mountains are incised with a maze of finger-like gorges. Esy, Virginia, and Andrea had been drawn into a canyon twisting east off the ridgeline. We chose a drainage that tended in a more northeasterly direction and luckily found the correct canyon. Above us to the northwest towered the 8,951-foot summit of Tin Mountain. The Cottonwood Mountains trap just enough moisture to allow a sparse stand of pinyon pines to inhabit the higher reaches. We quickly descended through the conifers, passed occasional Joshua trees, and after a few miles of hiking, dropped into the confines of Bighorn Gorge.

Each of Death Valley's canyons has its own character. Erosion of different rock types, the strike or slope of the mountains, the size of the drainage basin, age of the canyon, amounts of precipitation, exposure to freeze and thaw cycles, cracking and jointing patterns of the rock—and perhaps a host of factors we have never thought about—contribute to making each canyon unique and different from its neighbors. Bighorn Gorge proved to be a beautiful chasm. The gravelly canyon floor zigzagged between towering walls, narrowed to just a few feet across, then spilled over chutes of fluted and polished rock. Over most of the drop-offs we lowered our packs and cameras with the rope. Then, pressing against opposing walls with hands and legs, we would chimney our way down-occasionally finishing the descent by letting go, sliding like children at play.

The more serious dryfalls required route-finding around each obstruction. We came to one drop-off that fell fifty feet. We ventured to the edge for a look straight down into the pit. A good breeze blew through Bighorn Gorge that

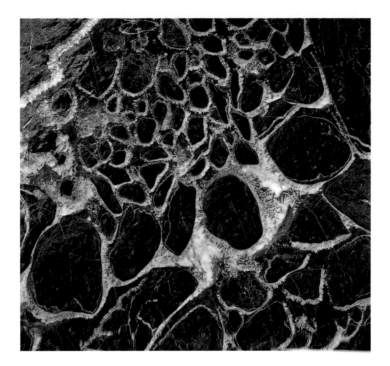

day, heralding a late winter cold front. Here, the canyon walls pulled together like the closing of a dragon's jaws. Wind, squeezed into the narrow passage, created howling gusts that felt like they would suck us off the slippery lip and fling us into the abyss below. We backtracked up canyon and to the north found a steep, rocky slope that held promise as a possible way around the impassable dryfall. Atop the ridge, we found an even steeper descent back to the canyon floor. The first fifty feet or so, little ball bearings of gravel peppered tiny ledges that sloped downward. Our rope provided an added measure of security, although finding a safe point to anchor was difficult.

The next section of the descent followed a huge scree slope where an entire portion of the mountain above had torn loose from its footing

Patterns in shattered carbonate breccia, wall of Bighorn Gorge.

Lichen creates colorful patterns on basalt boulders in the Nelson Range.

The abrasive force of such torrents not only excavated the hollowed chamber where we stood, but also cleanly carried away all the rock transported to the canyon bottom via the huge landslide we had just traversed. Despite the extreme aridity of Death Valley, before us was convincing evidence that *water* has been the master carver of this landscape.

We camped for the night, with cold canyon winds removing all trace of Death Valley's daytime warmth. Deep within Bighorn Gorge, our entire world encompassed the low bench where we rolled out our sleeping bags, the narrow gravel strip of the wash below us, and the gigantic canyon walls looming high above. With just a narrow sliver of sky visible, the Earth's rotation became apparent—all night long, stars quickly rose along a canyon wall, scurried across the opening, and set upon the opposite wall.

Dawn arrived cold and windy. To generate warmth and get our blood flowing, we broke camp early and commenced hiking. Bighorn Gorge had been spectacular, but the sights we soon encountered imparted memories to last a lifetime. We saw our first hint at what was to come, a weathered pair of fossil gastropods or snails poking from a dolomite ledge. Soon there were dozens, then hundreds, of gastropods appearing on the canyon walls, in sizes ranging from the diameter of a penny to that of a grapefruit. All were displayed in exquisite cross sections. The gorge was narrow enough that the rock on both sides next to the wash remained smoothed and polished by infrequent floods.

in a cataclysmic event and careened into the canyon. The sweeping pile of talus seemed so long and steep. Could the addition of our insignificant weight start it sliding again? Were we not like ants traversing a pile of sand where the ants' footwork triggers a sand slide? At least ants have hard exoskeletons to protect their bodies. We worked our way down through the boulders, landing on occasional teetering rocks that pumped our adrenaline, but otherwise found our way back to the canyon without mishap. Viewed from below, the dryfall was just as impressive as the sight we viewed so nervously from above. A great drapery of rock carved over the eons hung before us. We could visualize the tremendous cutting action of flash floods slicing through hard dolomitic limestone.

14

We journeyed deep into geologic time among fossilized remains of sea creatures who had lived during Ordovician times more than 450 million years ago.

Working with the 4x5 field cameras allowed us to study the fossils in intimate detail. The process of finding interesting scenes, setting up the camera, crawling beneath the dark cloth, and composing the shot on ground glass gave us time to closely observe nature's geologic bounty. Randi explains:

When I found the gastropods, I was mesmerized by their simple beauty. Calcified lines drew white images of intricate design. These ancient snails revealed a world vastly different from the Death Valley I knew. As I walked by hundreds of these fossils, I envisioned a land covered with an expansive sea, teeming with life, but ending in death. I was reminded of climate's powerful influence in charting the course of life on earth. Farther down canyon, I caught a glimpse of a fossil I almost passed by and knelt to gaze upon a perfect cross-section of a cephalopod embedded in the limestone. Enthralled, I lingered with this ancient relative of the nautilus, studying and photographing its symmetrical form until it too became embedded in my mind. How fortunate to gain a glimpse of life millions of years ago.

Beyond the walls of gastropods came more geologic wonders. Many of Death Valley's canyons expose faces of shattered carbonate breccia. This rather lengthy name describes rocks, which under the pressure and folding of mountain-building, break into fragments that later cement back together with white calcite. Bighorn Gorge contained splendid examples.

One of the wildest mosaics held shattered fragments that began with basketball-sized boulders and evenly graded down to rice-sized grains. We could only wonder about the titanic forces that created such an orderly jigsaw puzzle from the rock. We could have spent days in this canyon with our cameras, scrambling over rocks, exploring every little nook and cranny, poking our heads up a major side drainage and even searching for desert bighorn sheep. But explorations in Death Valley are limited by one essential element: water. The fact that we each carried about thirty-five pounds of camera gear limited how many days worth of water we could also haul. So before our throats became too parched, we left Bighorn Gorge and traversed the huge alluvial fan that would bring our

Stream orchis (Epipactis gigantea) *blooms in the riparian habitat of Surprise Canyon.*

The highly adaptable and intelligent raven (Corvus corax) thrives in Death Valley. This same species can withstand the 120°F heat of the California deserts and the −60°F cold of Arctic Alaska.

journey to an end at Mesquite Springs.

The final leg of our hike entailed a four-mile passage across Tin Mountain's *bajada*, the broad slope formed by coalescence of numerous alluvial fans and dry stream beds. The traverse felt longer as we climbed up and down countless drainages. Pink spines covering healthy clumps of cotton-top cactus provided splashes of color along the way. We encountered many basalt boulders coated with a dark patina of desert varnish. Long ago, floods had transported these volcanic rocks from lava flows on the flank of Tin Mountain. On just a handful of these boulders, we found the ancient workings of Death Valley's original Shoshonean inhabitants. Their petroglyphs featured a variety of geometric squiggles, sun designs, circles, and grids, pecked into the dark varnish with rock tools. Similar rock carvings across the Great Basin are often found near springs or in canyons where game animals likely traveled. In the vastness of Death Valley's desert, rock art is uncommon. When we do find petroglyphs and pictographs, we wonder about the people who lived here hundreds of years ago. They successfully made the dry land their home—and some of their descendants continue to do so—attesting to their adaptability, skills, and intellect. We know from our photographic work in Death Valley how challenging this desert can be. But our difficulties were minimal compared to those of earlier people. Randi mused:

> *We purchased our food, clothing, and footware from stores—they hunted, gathered food, and made clothing from the desert's plants and animals. We conveniently filled our water bottles from a tap while they knew which of Death Valley's nearly four hundred springs were safe to drink.*

Toward the end of our Bighorn Gorge hike, Randi's feet began to swell and hurt. She loosened her leather hiking boots and told me:

> *Think about the people who hand-made their sandals and walked hundreds of miles across these canyons and alluvial fans. I marvel at the tenacity of Death Valley's Timbisha Shoshone people to forge a living in North America's driest and hottest place.*

After two days not seeing a human soul besides ourselves, we wandered into the bustle of Mesquite Springs Campground and found our truck parked by the friends who had so graciously dropped us off on the top of Cottonwood Mountain. We popped open cold drinks, rested sore feet, and unfolded the map to choose our next hiking adventure, confident that Death Valley National Park's 3.3 million acres allow incredible options of places to explore. We drifted off to sleep resting assured that no matter where we wandered within the park, we were bound to discover new treasures.

The California Desert Protection Act of 1994 added Saline Valley to Death Valley National Park. At an elevation of 1,073 feet above sea level, Salt Lake on the floor of Saline Valley stands 1,355 higher than the lowest point in neighboring Death Valley.

Sunrise light illuminates the Confidence Hills and Owlshead Mountains, viewed from The Narrows of Death Valley.

Opposite: A double rainbow follows a spring shower north of Furnace Creek.

East away from the Sierras, south from Panamint and Amargosa, east and south many an uncounted mile, is the Country of Lost Borders.

> —Mary Austin,
> The Land of Little Rain *(1903)*

DEATH VALLEY NATIONAL PARK:
AN ENVIRONMENTAL HISTORY

by Mark A. Schlenz

Desert landscapes have always challenged and inspired human imagination. Throughout history they have been refuges for renegades, frontiers for fortune-seekers, and places of inspiration for prophets and poets. When Mary Hunter Austin first arrived in California's deserts at the end of the nineteenth century, earlier European arrivals had done much in less than half a century to displace native cultures and ecological systems that had flourished in these lands for ages before them. As she struggled herself for survival on an arid homestead, Austin witnessed both the destructive effects of human exploitation on desert lands and native peoples *and* their resilient integrity even in the face of civilization's onslaught. Giving poetic expression in her literary works to the struggles for existence that she witnessed

and experienced in and around the regions of Death Valley, Mary Austin prophesized that these lands would eventually come to hold new meaning for our modern world and critical significance for our continued survival.

A Country of Lost Borders

One of the desert's earliest and most eloquent advocates, Mary Austin called the Death Valley region a "Country of Lost Borders," where, she wrote, "…not the law, but the land sets the limit." In her 1903 classic, *The Land of Little Rain*, she explained that "Out there the boundary of soul and sense is faint as a trail in a sand-storm." Nearly a century later, though human impacts have continued to threaten the natural integrity of the region, earth-shaping forces and interactions of wind and water that

High in the Panamint Range, the Wildrose Charcoal Kilns still carry an aroma of burnt wood resin. Built in 1876 to make charcoal for the smelting furnaces of the Modoc mine, the kilns operated only a few years before mining fortunes changed.

Photographic images within this book present glimpses of incredible natural beauty and ecological richness protected within the boundaries of Death Valley National Park. They also invite further consideration of long-range ecological and administrative implications of the act's newly-drawn borders in California's desert lands—implications that may forever influence natural and environmental histories of Death Valley and its region.

Presidential proclamations by Herbert Hoover in 1933 and by Franklin Roosevelt in 1937 established and expanded Death Valley National Monument. The initial proclamation created the monument for "the preservation of the unusual features of scenic, scientific, and educational interests therein contained." In the six decades between establishment of Death Valley National Monument and its redesignation as a national park in 1994, natural, ecological, and wilderness values have gathered critical environmental importance. And increased support for sound ecological management of these deserts has successfully challenged less protective multiple-use designations.

ultimately define conditions of life and death in the desert have continued to transcend human influences and inspire our human spirit. Today, more recent efforts of mapmakers and lawmakers to establish boundaries "out there" promise to exert more enlightened influences on the region's landscapes and ecologies.

In 1994, The California Desert Protection Act extended boundaries and redesignated environmental protection of public lands in the Death Valley region. The act erased the old borders of the former Death Valley National Monument and established 3.3 million-acre Death Valley National Park. In this "Country of Lost Borders," lines marking the disestablished national monument have faded from maps and from the land itself. Just as quickly, new horizons of opportunity and challenge for natural resource management and public enjoyment opened by the California Desert Protection Act in Death Valley National Park have taken on dramatic focus.

While laws set the boundaries of federally-protected land, our own imaginative responses to these deserts' appealing and scenic beauty inspire us to argue concern for their preservation. Literature and art in defense of natural beauty have long been powerful allies of ecological and wilderness values. The 1950 reissue of *The Land of Little Rain* joins Mary Austin's text with photographs of Death Valley and surrounding regions by Ansel Adams. Stories of the land—told by those who have known it intimately and passionately—provide an indispensible forum for building public support for environmental protection of public lands in America. During congressional debates, Austin's desert descriptions in *The Land of Little Rain* were echoed to inspire passage of the California Desert Protection Act. As he addressed the Senate, the Secretary of the Interior stated that

> *anyone who raises the argument that this land is not special or not of park quality or not significant should simply be handed a copy of that book and requested to read the introduction where she speaks of the rainbow hills, the tender blue mists, the luminous radiance of spring.*

By presenting images of dramatic scenic beauty and insights into natural processes that bring those landscapes to life, photoessayists promote preservation of fragile lands. Joining images and stories of these deserts in this book, Fred and Randi Hirschmann document an historic moment in environmental preservation through celebration of the scenic and natural wonder protected within the expanded boundaries of Death Valley National Park. Their art invites us to deepen our imaginative responses to California's desert wildlands and to give even deeper consideration to the significance of the lines we draw on our maps and to their impacts upon the natural world that surrounds us.

Drawing the Boundaries

Severe climate and terrain stymied nineteenth-century surveyors in and around Death Valley. Presumably European explorers had not

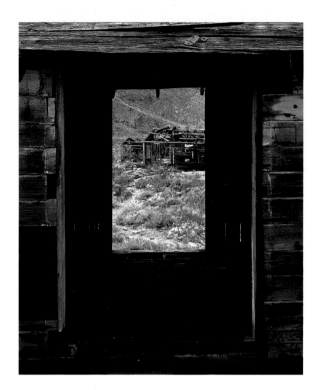

seen the the valley's depths in 1846 when the treaty of Guadalupe Hildalgo transferred the region from Mexico to the United States. Horse traders and thieves, however, had been running herds over the route called *jornada del muerto*—journey of death—through the Amargosa country since the 1830s.

In 1848 John C. Fremont mapped an illusory east-west transverse range through the desert country. Unfortunate argonauts seeking a cut-off route to California's goldfields in 1849 had followed mountains they supposed to be those on Fremont's map. Their misjudgment led them away from the Old Spanish Trail—and the narrows and springs of the Amargosa Valley—directly into the Amargosa River's deep, bitter sink. William Manly and John Rogers struck out

Weathered ruins at the Inyo Mine in Echo Canyon record Death Valley's boom and bust mining days. Active gold mining occurred here from 1905 to 1907 and again between 1928 and 1940.

Periods of heavy rain occasionally flood the Death Valley salt pan. Dry desert air evaporates the briny solution and redeposits the dissolved salts.

ing, without success, a transcontinental-railroad route. A year later, Fremont made the final expedition of his career, only to meet disappointment in Death Valley country when he failed to find the by-now fabled east-west dividing range.

The United States Congress had set the California-Nevada state line—a diagonal from the Colorado River to Lake Tahoe—in 1850, and California claimed desert lands east of the Sierra. Miners in the Nevada Territory, however, countered with claims that their western boundary should reach to the Sierra's crest. The California Boundary Commission sent forth a survey expedition to settle the dispute—on imported camels, the last remnants of Jefferson Davis' ill-fated Camel Corps. The camels, while well-suited for travel across sand, proved less reliable than mules in the steep terrain of the Death Valley region. Although unable to settle the border dispute, the expedition did make the first scientific measurements of the valley's below-sea-level elevations.

The Nevada legislature officially recognized California's claim to its eastern deserts in 1865. Yet by 1871 a definitive state boundary survey had not been completed. In the hot summer of that year young lieutenant George M. Wheeler entered Death Valley on the first major expedition of his illustrious career as an explorer of the West. Wheeler's party included scientists and naturalists as well as topographers, a photographer, and a poet. The group produced maps of the area despite the stupefying heat. Two guides disappeared under mysterious circumstances, joining the ranks of lost men in Death Valley

on foot for help, returning after a 26-day heroic traverse of rugged desert to lead their fellow travelers out of the valley known ever after for the near-fatal tragedy that befell them there.

The name "Death Valley" first appeared in print in an 1861 newspaper account describing a return visit by Manly and surviving Forty-Niners to the scene of their travail. Sensational stories about the desert appeared in newspapers, magazines, and dime novels—eagerly absorbed by Americans thirsty for news of the West. This intractable, vast country became a land of legend as well as lost borders.

As legends grew, map-makers sought to establish new borders and new routes through the Death Valley region. The first official surveyors had entered the valley in 1853 seek-

legend. Wheeler himself never returned to these deserts in his later explorations.

Alexey Von Schmidt's 1856 Panamint Valley survey for the General Land Office was denounced as shameless fraud by the California Boundary Commission. When Von Schmidt finally completed a survey of the line from Lake Tahoe to the Colorado River in 1873, its validity was also quickly questioned. Walter Scott, "Death Valley Scotty," first came to the region with a survey crew sent in the 1890s to straighten out Von Schmidt's California–Nevada demarcation. Ironically, adjustments for errors in the Von Schmidt survey led to property disputes over Scotty's Castle decades later when Death Valley National Monument was established in 1933.

Death Valley Scotty never actually owned the castle, though he certainly held court there— spinning fantastic yarns for gullible guests and enjoying the largesse of his friend and benefactor, Chicago magnate Albert Johnson. Scotty was perhaps a better storyteller than prospector, although he often hinted about a secret gold mine of his own. Survey adjustments revealed that Johnson had actually claimed land more than a mile from where they were building their legendary desert retreat. The Park Service allowed Johnson to buy back the land beneath his architectural extravagance, but the Great Depression broke Johnson's fortune and his palatial, hacienda dreams. Today the Park Service preserves Scotty's Castle in its unfinished splendor, and Death Valley Scotty's legends live on to lure desert travelers still seeking boom and bust glories of a by-gone era.

Among late-nineteenth- and early-twentieth-century miners and fortune seekers who followed the early explorers and mapmakers into Death Valley, naturalists and scientists also sought discoveries in the desert. In 1893 the Death Valley Expedition published official biological surveys of the region for the U. S. Department of Agriculture. Death Valley's varied terrain provided expedition scientists unique opportunities to study geographic distributions of flora and fauna. From mud-covered salt flats below sea level at Badwater to limber and bristlecone pine forests high in the Panamints, an elevation gain of nearly twelve thousand feet dramatically exposes seven distinct life-zones. The Death Valley Expedition's findings stimulated further scientific study

Sunrise illuminates the Last Chance Mountains, viewed from Last Chance Canyon at the extreme northern end of Death Valley. The California Desert Protection Act added this remote region to the park and created the Piper Mountain and Sylvania Mountain Wilderness Areas on adjacent Bureau of Land Management holdings.

In the parched desert air, showers often fall as virga—evaporating before they hit the ground. Only the rare major rainstorm actually waters the desert.

borax out of the valley behind twenty-mule teams switched to skinning bucks from tourists drawn by accounts of scenic wonder and tales of Old West adventure. Soon the tourist bonanza led to proposals for a Death Valley National Park—proposals which further dramatized difficulties of drawing boundaries in the desert.

In the 1920s mining interests prevented a national park bill from reaching Congress. Finally, Herbert Hoover established Death Valley National Monument by presidential proclamation in 1933. As a presidentially-established monument rather than congressionally-designated park, Death Valley was protected under the American Antiquities Act of 1906. This act protected romantically-rusted relics of late-nineteenth- and early-twentieth-century mining equipment for their "unusual features of scenic, scientific, and educational interests." It also left the monument open to continued mineral prospecting and extraction. Fortunately, fragile desert habitats and uniquely-adapted plant and animal species also received significant protection in Death Valley National Monument. So too did evidence of more subtle natural and human environmental histories inscribed upon the land.

A Land of Little Rain

Despite Death Valley's dryness, humans have occupied this region for thousands of years. Near scattered springs native peoples etched images into the varnished surfaces of boulders. We may only imagine the world-views

of the valley's "climatic violence" and dispelled many fantastical myths about its natural history. Chief among these was the myth of the valley's lifelessness. As the expedition catalogued new species of poppies, pupfish, lizards, and the desert bighorn sheep *(Ovis canadensis nelsoni)* it became obvious that Death Valley teemed with lifeforms awaiting discovery.

Surveyors and topographers prepared the way for roadbuilders and entirely new modes of desert travel. Intense heat and vast waterless distances challenged nineteenth-century explorers and pioneers, but the entrance of the automobile—and then the airplane—into Death Valley finally defeated those obstacles. In the 1920s, men who had made fortunes driving

mapped by prehistoric petroglyphs and appreciate the skill and patience used to create them. Perhaps the mysterious stone markings represented visions of a successful hunt, or propitiated the spirits of the game; perhaps they expressed the people's experience of their environment. Today ecologists interpret artful depictions of desert bighorn sheep as archaeological evidence of this critically endangered species' prehistoric ranges. While rock art may invite imaginative interpretations of ancient lifeways, other lines etched into the landscape relate directly to survival in these desert lands.

Old trails tell timeless tales of the search for water—they often mark the most direct routes between springs. Converging coyote and animal tracks may also show the direction to closest water. Prehistoric stone fire rings and flint artifacts found along the trails speak of human passages over these routes throughout the ages. Rusted relics and litter along the way tell the history of nineteenth- and twentieth-century travelers and prospectors. Since establishment of the monument, only small animals and perhaps occasional hikers use the old trails. Through the decades, inexorable geologic and hydrologic forces have slowly begun to erase these human traces. Using comparative studies of old trails as baselines, geologists can measure erosional rates on the Valley's alluvial fans.

The constant quest for water defines even more subtle landscape patterns. Overlapping and distinct boundaries of vegetation zones and particular distributions of plant and animal species may provide the desert's truest map.

In *The Land of Little Rain*, Mary Austin wrote:

> *...the true desert breeds its own kind, each in its particular habitat. The angle of the slope, the frontage of a hill, the structure of the soil determines the plant. South-looking hills are nearly bare, and the lower tree-line higher here by a thousand feet. Cañons running east and west will have one wall naked and one clothed. Around dry lakes and marshes the herbage preserves a set and orderly arrangement. Most species have well-defined areas of growth, the best index the voiceless land can give the traveler of his whereabouts.*

In this arid region, the particular plants found in any area, their relative size, and their proximity to each other give mute testimony to the availability of moisture and ground water.

A coyote (Canis latrans) *patiently waits for a meal on an alluvial fan of Death Valley. Coyotes are opportunistic feeders. Their success, in part, rests upon their ability to devour a wide variety of foods.*

Notch-leaf phacelia (Phacelia crenulata) *and golden evening primrose* (Camissonia brevipes) *carpet Echo Canyon's alluvial fan following a particularly wet winter.*

bristlecone. Across this hydrologically articulated floral mosaic, small and large mammals, birds, reptiles, and even fish live in uniquely adapted forms and patterns of life.

Death Valley's animals have widely varying geographic ranges. An endemic pupfish species may occupy a single remote spring; Costa's hummingbirds migrate from the desert to the coast each summer to escape the desert heat. Resident and migratory species often possess physical and behavioral adaptations to the desert's habitats. Many mammals and raptors—kit foxes, kangaroo rats, and burrowing owls—are primarily nocturnal, sleeping through the scorching days. Most cold blooded reptiles are more active during the day, warming their bodies with desert heat. But the rarely-seen banded gecko—with its soft, translucent skin—is uniquely suited for hunting during relatively cooler desert nights. Another elusive species, the desert bighorn sheep, has a complex digestive system that allows it to feed on tough desert vegetation unavailable to other herbivores. Bighorns travel great distances to waterholes and approach them warily to avoid predators. Fortunately the sheep can rehydrate quickly after losing up to a fifth of their body weight in moisture.

Re-Drawing the Boundaries

For aeons, complex interactions of flora and fauna have evolved an interdependent kaleidoscope of life and land in Death Valley. Early human occupants depended upon their

Xeric plants—desert holly, creosote, and beavertail cactus—survive on alluvial fans where the water table lies too far below the surface for roots to reach. Creosote grows noticeably larger and more abundantly along roadsides where run-off from infrequent desert rain concentrates. Other plants—such as mesquite—send roots to the water table. Willows and reed grass may mark locations of springs. Plants adapted to hypersaline water—such as arrowweed, salt-bush, saltgrass, and pickleweed —ring salt-encrusted mudflats. Colorful ephemeral wild-flowers paint desert hillsides in response to annual rainfall variations. In the surrounding mountain heights, seasonal snows water conifer-ous forests of pinyon, juniper, limber pine, and

understanding of the desert's subtly shifting patterns. More recent arrivals have fixed more arbitrary boundaries. In the century-and-a-half since pioneers first entered the intractable frontiers of the Californian deserts, map makers have charted the entire region with complicated overlays of property and jurisdiction divisions. Survey-marker grids, section-line roads, barbed-wire fences, railroad grades, pipeline tunnels, concrete aqueducts, high-voltage towers, and six-lane interstates score these divisions into the earth itself. This sectioning has devastating effects on the deserts' ecologies—and make protecting our remaining desert wildlands increasingly critical. Perhaps Death Valley National Park's intrinsic beauty, its integrity of natural processes, and its still vital wholeness may yet provide insights for our own continued survival.

Mining, road building, railroads, water and power reclamation projects, military training and weapons testing, nuclear testing, nuclear and other toxic waste storage, and sprawling subur-ban development have fragmented and degraded many desert ecologies in regions surrounding Death Valley National Monument since its establishment in 1933. The addition of wilder-ness lands to the former monument and its redesignation as Death Valley National Park by the California Desert Protection Act of 1994 make vital contributions to the preservation of our remaining desert wildlands.

With an added 1.3 million acres, Death Valley National Park protects an area half again as extensive as the former monument. It is now

the largest national park in the contiguous United States. In addition to expanding and redesignating Death Valley National Park, the California Desert Protection Act also enlarged and redesignated Joshua Tree National Monument as Joshua Tree National Park. Both new parks share boundaries with wilderness areas administered by the Bureau of Land Management. In the region between Death Valley and Joshua Tree National Parks the act also established Mojave National Preserve to protect "the particular ecosystems and transi-tional desert type found in the Mojave desert between them."

The California Desert Protection Act may have created Death Valley National Park's

Telescope Peak (el. 11,049 feet), the highest point in Death Valley National Park, reflects in the pool at Badwater, 279 feet below sea level. Just a few miles away, the Death Valley sink drops to 282 feet below sea level, the lowest point in the park as well as North America.

Sunset illuminates Bald Peak, as viewed from south of Nemo Crest in the Panamint Range.

management of the region's natural resources and wilderness values.

As the twenty-first century begins, ecological management of Death Valley National Park will require expanded public environmental awareness based upon sustained research and monitoring. More and more people in the cities and suburbs surrounding California's deserts must understand how these landscapes fit into the geographies and histories of their lives. If we and our world's natural wonders are to survive challenges of human growth, we must extend our imagination to encompass more than just the scenic beauty of dramatic landforms. We must also comprehend more subtle beauties of myriad lifeforms these lands embrace. And we must remove borders we imagine between our world and theirs, between their fate and ours. Fortunately, as Mary Austin and other artist-naturalists in this country of lost borders have long known, desert landscapes themselves can inspire such salutary expansion of our human imagination. The desert horizons' liberating distance—and the rejuvenating intimacy of desert skies—naturally erase illusory boundaries we draw between ourselves and infinity; they invite us eternally to recreate ourselves anew:

> *For all the toll the desert takes…it gives compensations, deep breaths, deep sleep, and the communion of the stars.*
>
> —*Mary Austin,* The Land of Little Rain

newly-drawn boundaries, but it still allows substantial compromises to mining interests. The Act also allows continued and unrestricted military use of desert air space, including low-level overflights of Death Valley National Park and adjacent wilderness areas. Less than a hundred miles to the east of the park boundary, the federal government plans "permanent storage" of high-grade plutonium waste at Yucca Mountain in Nevada. Nearby Las Vegas is one of the fastest growing metropolitan areas in America, and the not-so-distant cities of coastal California are already among the largest metropolitan areas in the world. Increasing human population pressures present ever-larger and more complicated challenges to ecological

Death Valley National Park's 3.3 million acres contain many treasures. Although the landscape may appear barren, sequestered in the Grapevine Mountains are hidden springs, shaded canyons, and colorful rock formations.

In the 1970s this fragile natural area was slated to become an off-road vehicle playground. Botanist Mary DeDecker fought a long and successful battle to preserve the Eureka Sand Dunes, and this outstanding ecosystem was added to Death Valley National Park in 1994 by the California Desert Protection Act.

Eureka Dunes evening primrose (Oenothera californica *ssp.* eurekensis) *is one of three extremely rare endemic plants found growing only in the Eureka Sand Dunes. Death Valley National Park harbors over fifty different species of endemic plants—which grow only in the vicinity of the park and nowhere else in the world.*

31

The 1.3 million acres of land added to Death Valley National Park in October, 1994 included most of remote Saline Valley, now the park's northwest corner. Among boulders in the southern end of this magnificent basin, Mojave aster (Xylorhiza tortifolia) *blooms in spring.*

The dunes of Saline Valley encompass five square miles of rolling, sandy dune formations. To the west, the rugged Inyo Mountains rise nearly two miles above the valley floor.

Although the floor of Saline Valley is scorching hot on summer days, liquid water is always present. The nearby Inyo Mountains capture a considerable amount of moisture over the course of a year that reappears at seeps and springs on the valley floor. At least 124 species of birds utilize the perennial supply of water at Saline Valley Marsh.

Saltgrass (Distichlis spicta) *and pickleweed* (Salicornia rubra) *are two salt-tolerant plants thriving along the shoreline of Salt Lake in Saline Valley. Plentiful spring water once supported the nearby Timbisha Shoshone village of Ko-o, which had a population of 125 people.*

The sandy pages of a dunes story book—soon to be erased by afternoon winds—tell of a congregation of ravens (Corvus corax) *walking over the Saline Valley Dunes in search of insects and other food. Shifting sands may appear lifeless at first glance, but upon closer inspection teem with life.*

Migrating American avocets (Recurvirostra americana) *find a haven in the shallow water of Saline Valley's Salt Lake.*
They use their long, slightly upturned bills to probe mud for aquatic food. Water-loving birds, including common loons, white
pelicans, double-crested cormorants, ospreys, ducks, and geese have also been observed in Death Valley National Park.

Granite outcrops in the Nelson Range rise beyond a grove of Joshua trees (Yucca brevifolia) *near the upper reaches of Lee Flat. In the Death Valley region, Joshua trees typically grow at elevations of 3,500 to 6,000 feet. A female moth of the genus* Tegeticula *pollinates Joshua trees when she lays each egg in the ovary of individual flowers. As the Joshua tree seeds mature, the moth's caterpillars are assured a steady supply of nourishment while the tree benefits from having a reliable pollinator.*

A pair of brown-headed cowbirds (Molothrus ater) *rest atop a blooming Joshua tree during their spring migration. Cowbirds parasitize a variety of songbirds—they lay their eggs in others species' nests, and have surrogate parents raise their young.*

A granite outcrop called The Grandstand rises from the cracked mud of the Racetrack playa. This island on the dry lake surface represents just the tip of a mountain almost completely buried by alluvium and lake-bed sediments.

The Racetrack playa's "moving rocks" remain a fascinating mystery. Zigzagging and curved trails trace each boulder's meandering journey across the playa. This phenomenon occurs on a small number of dry lake beds in the desert southwest, although no person has actually seen the rocks move.

Why do rocks on the Racetrack move? Theories abound. High winds and a wet or frosted playa surface are probably prerequisites to start the rocks sliding. Perhaps the most likely scenario involves heavy winter rains flooding the playa, followed by freezing temperatures creating ice which imbeds the rocks. Then strong winds break the ice apart and raft the rocks along on ice floes, scraping their trails in the slick, wet mud.

42

Ubehebe Peak's 5,678-foot summit reflects in still water covering the Racetrack playa. Death Valley National Park's lakes are ephemeral in nature, lasting only days or weeks before drying in the parched desert air.

Vegetation typical of the Great Basin desert covers the floor of Hidden Valley near Lost Burro Gap. Successive mountain ranges to the west, culminating in the Sierra Nevada, wring moisture from storms moving eastward off the Pacific Ocean. The entire park lies in a rain shadow.

Moisture trapped by the lofty peaks of the Panamint Range allows pinyon pines (Pinus monophylla) *to grow above approximately 6,200 feet in elevation. Similar tree islands occur at high elevations on Last Chance Mountain, Hunter Mountain, and in the Cottonwood and Grapevine Mountains.*

Brilliant blossoms of Englemann's hedgehog cactus (Echinocereus engelmannii) *decorate alluvial fans from March through early June, with most flowering occuring in April. Even in the driest of years, cactus store enough moisture to produce showy blooms amid the sharp thorns.*

A clump of young cottontop cactus (Echinocactus polycephalus) *grows from cracks in a limestone outcrop in Warm Springs Canyon. As cottontops mature, they produce small light yellow flowers on the tops of the cactus heads. The fruits that follow are enveloped in rounded cottony tufts of hair.*

Spring lightning strikes a hilltop beyond the 1,500 fenced acres of Death Valley Ranch. From 1915 to 1927, insurance magnate Albert Johnson acquired remote land in Grapevine Canyon where he built an elaborate home—known to most Death Valley National Park visitors as Scotty's Castle.

No detail was left untouched in building Scotty's Castle, a 12,000-square-foot Spanish Provincial mansion and associated outbuildings. A tile bird house sits atop the original gas station on the castle grounds. Although some of the ornate tiles used within the elaborate home may have been imported from Spain, most were handmade in Southern California.

Death Valley Wash flows with water for a short time after rainstorms, then quickly dries. As mud carried downstream slowly dessicates, cracking patterns of infinite variety develop. In this arid land, rain erodes the grandest of landscapes and also helps create the most intimate geologic decorations.

A departing storm embraces the Grapevine Mountains as the late afternoon sun bathes the sand dunes near Stovepipe Wells in contrasting light. This fifteen-square-mile dune field is the largest in Death Valley National Park. Each passing windstorm rearranges billions of sand grains, mostly eroded from the nearby Cottonwood Mountains.

In wetter times during the last ice age, a series of large lakes occupied what is now Death Valley National Park. Today, only heavy rains and mountain snowmelt temporarily spread water across these ancient basins. This ephemeral lake occupying Panamint Valley was once fed by water overflowing Searles Lake and a string of lakes stretching up the east side of the Sierra Nevada.

On the average, the floor of Death Valley receives less than two inches of rain annually—making it the driest place in the United States. When rains do come, they can be torrential. Following a flash flood spawned by a nighttime thunderstorm, frothy water collects in depressions around the Death Valley Sand Dunes.

Just the right combination of winter rains dispersed from October through March triggers superb spring blooms. A desert mariposa (Calochortus kennedyi) *brings a splash of orange to Saline Valley in April.*

SPRINGTIME IN DEATH VALLEY

Clockwise from upper left: Rare, endemic Panamint daisy (Enceliopsis covillei); *perennial brittlebush* (Encelia farinosa); *rocknettle* (Eucnide urens); *and endemic Panamint stonecrop* (Dudleya saxosa *ssp.* saxosa).

The salt pan of Death Valley consists mainly of common table salt (Sodium chloride) *with smaller quantities of other salts and silt. Leached from the surrounding mountains over the eons, the salt precipitated from drying Lake Manly, which filled the valley during the Ice Age. Lake Manly may have measured a hundred miles long, six to eleven miles wide, and six hundred feet deep.*

The floor of a lake predating Pleistocene Lake Manly produced the fine-grained muds and siltstones that have eroded into colorful badlands viewed from Zabriskie Point. Virtually no vegetation grows in the deeply furrowed landscape incised into the northern edge of the Black Mountains.

A lone plant of salt-tolerant pickleweed (Salicornia rubra) *grows on the badlands near Salt Creek.*
Although the land may seem devoid of vegetation, more than one thousand species, subspecies, or varieties
of plants occur within Death Valley National Park's boundaries.

The roots and branches of Arrowweed (Pluches sericea) *capture wind-blown sand to create unusual mounds at the Devils Cornfield. Arrowweed grows in close proximity to underground water and tolerates alkalinity.*

Fog fills Wildrose Canyon as fresh snow covers the pinyon pine-studded slopes of Rogers Peak. At 8,133 feet, Mahogany Flat experiences wintry conditions from October to April. In summer, the crest of the Panamint Range offers a cool respite from the intense heat of the valley floor.

Warm air cooling as it rises over the crest of the Panamint Range near Aguereberry Point wrings additional moisture from the typically dry desert air. Vegetation increases up slope and eventually culminates in coniferous forest. Ridge lines and mountain tops in the basin and range province provide sky islands of moister habitat.

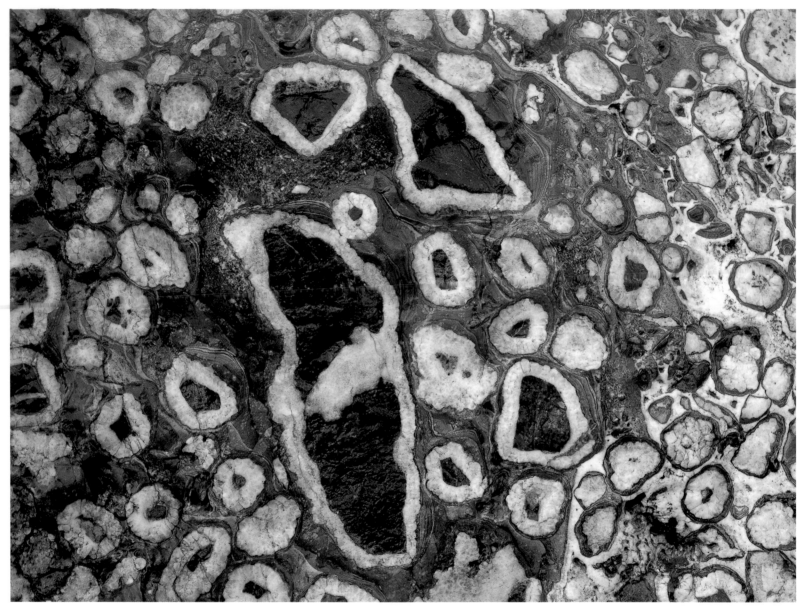

Flash floods grind and polish the walls of Death Valley canyons, revealing geologic designs of intricate beauty. In a narrows of Cottonwood Canyon, a shattered limestone wall is filled with calcite geodes and vugs.

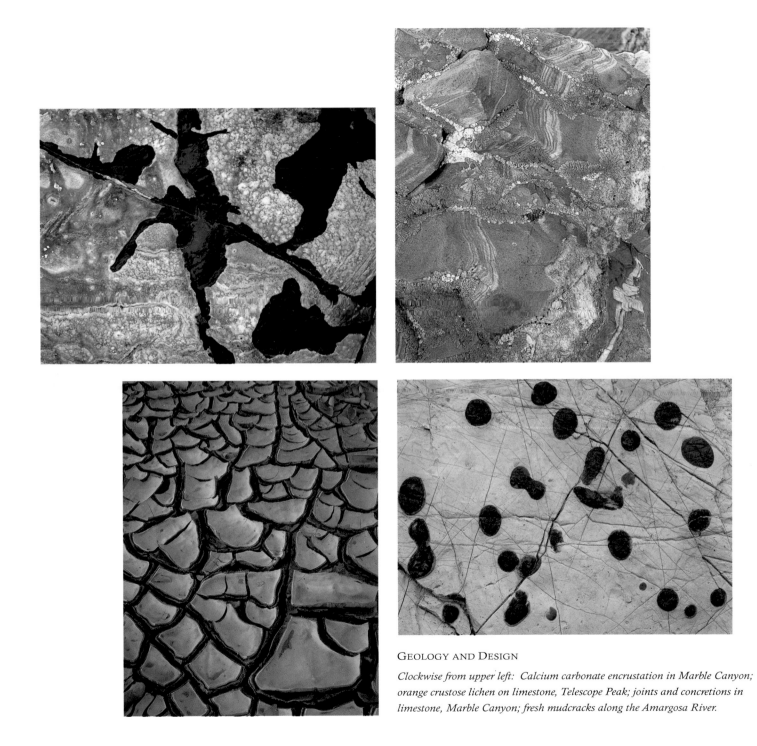

GEOLOGY AND DESIGN

Clockwise from upper left: Calcium carbonate encrustation in Marble Canyon; orange crustose lichen on limestone, Telescope Peak; joints and concretions in limestone, Marble Canyon; fresh mudcracks along the Amargosa River.

One of the gems in the extreme southern end of Death Valley, the Ibex Dunes form the smallest dune field in the park. Covering just two square miles with shifting sand, their undulating crest rises 160 feet. To the east of the Saddle Peak Hills and just outside the park stand the Dumont Dunes.

The Amargosa River drains about 6,000 square miles of land in the southern half of Death Valley and beyond. The river is usually a dry wash along its course, but following heavy rains, it discharges water into the 200-square-mile Death Valley playa.

Some of Death Valley's canyons are exceedingly narrow and convoluted. Light fails to penetrate their innermost depths, so hikers may require a flashlight to explore them. Flash floods careening through weakly-cemented alluvial deposits carve the sinuous chambers.

Only a handful of perennial waterfalls exist in Death Valley National Park. Deep in the Black Mountains, this ribbon of fresh water is a favorite haunt for the elusive desert bighorn sheep (Ovis canadensis nelsoni).

Deep in the narrows of Bighorn Gorge, stream-polished Pogonip Dolomite reveals cross-sections of hundreds of fossilized gastropods. These ancient snails lived during the Ordovician Period some 430 to 500 million years ago.

A desert horned lizard (Phrynosoma platyrhinos) *appears nearly perfectly camouflaged against a granite boulder in Cottonwood Canyon. Ants are a favorite prey of this secretive reptile.*

A petroglyph in a Nelson Range canyon depicts a desert bighorn sheep with young. Although this rock carving is more recent in origin, the oldest archaeological evidence of projectile points and hide scrapers indicates humans occupied Death Valley at least 10,000 years ago. Over the millenia, bighorn sheep have played an important role in the diet of Death Valley's early inhabitants.

Above a tinaja *or natural waterhole in the Greenwater Mountains, a shallow cave incised in soft volcanic rock may have served as a ceremonial shrine. The bedrock mortar or grinding hole and elaborate polychrome paintings of sheep, deer, humans, and geometric forms are unusual for the Death Valley region.*

Rock art in the Great Basin usually consists of abstract geometric forms of straight and curved lines. Drawings of bighorn sheep and human figures also appear on panels. In Death Valley, rock art may be found near springs, within canyons, or on isolated alluvial fan boulders. Although it is not possible to ascribe specific meaning to the rock art panels, many may be associated with hunting rituals.

Three looming figures or anthropomorphs with highly decorated bodies dominate the basalt wall of a Nelson Range canyon. Also depicted on the panel are numerous bighorn sheep. Some forty miles to the south of this site, three basalt-lined canyons on the China Lake Naval Weapons Station hold thousands of similar though typically more ornate petroglyphs.

In the southern portion of Death Valley National Park, Striped Butte rises from the floor of Butte Valley with a vertical strike to its layers of Paleozoic limestone. The mountains and valleys of the park result from the earth's crust being broken into a series of tilted blocks which have slipped past one another to create basin and range topography.

Saratoga Springs, near the southern border of Death Valley, is the only home for the rare Saratoga Springs pupfish (Cyprinondon nevadensis *ssp.* nevadensis). *The pools also provide sustenance for at least 150 species of birds, fifteen kinds of reptiles and amphibians, and eighteen types of mammals.*

On a talus slope above Arrastre Spring, a claret cup or mound cactus (Echinocereus triglochidiatus) *blooms in April. This variety of hedgehog cactus prefers uplands and mountains bordering valley deserts. Large rounded mounds may hold a hundred spine-covered stems.*

On the slopes of the Owlshead Mountains, burrobrush or bur-sage (Ambrosia dumosa) *and creosotebush* (Larrea tridentata) *wait for rain in a state of semi-dormancy. Burros and desert bighorn sheep have been known to graze on the bitter but aromatic burrobrush. Creosotebush tastes so disagreeable it escapes grazing, but smells fragrant following a rain.*

Petroglyphs of geometric shield designs and a spiral slowly fill with lichens on the limestone wall of a canyon incised on the west side of the Panamint Range. In arid climates, it usually takes hundreds of years for lichens to grow—this rock art may be many hundreds of years old.

Brilliant yellow crustose lichen decorates the wall of Hanaupah Canyon on the east side of the Panamints. Lichens represent a symbiotic relationship of algae and fungus living together as one organism. They help break down rocks and start building soils for other plant life.

93

Spectacular blooms—when Death Valley's alluvial fans wear lush carpets of wildflowers—occur only a few times each century. Following more than five inches of rain spread over the winter of 1997–98, desert gold (Geraea canescens) painted the rocky fields north of Furnace Creek a brilliant yellow.

Salt Creek drains the northwest arm of Death Valley, an area of about 2,200 square miles. Water flowing underground through Mesquite Flats and the Death Valley Sand Dunes meets impermeable beds of the Furnace Creek formation and then travels on the surface. The perennial stream enters the Death Valley Salt Pan at 240 feet below sea level. Here, briny water evaporates, returning scant moisture to the atmosphere.

Comet Hale-Bopp shines brightly in the crystalline air above the Racetrack during its 1997 spring visit. Hopefully Death Valley National Park will have just as clear air and pristine desert wilderness to explore when Hale-Bopp returns in 2,380 years for its AD 4377 appearance.

PHOTOGRAPHERS' NOTES

With a touch of humor, we refer to ourselves as a "two Toyo family." For photographing grand landscapes, we carry a pair of Toyo 45AII field cameras mounted on sturdy Gitzo tripods with Arca Swiss B-I monoballs. Randi's favorite 4x5-inch format lenses include the 90mm f 4.5 Nikkor-SW, 135mm f 5.6 Nikkor-W, 210mm f 5.6 Fujinon, and 300mm f 9 Nikkor-M. Lenses Fred prefers working with include the 75mm f 4.5 Nikkor-SW, 120mm f 5.6 Schneider Super-Symmar HM, 180mm f 5.6 Rodenstock Apo-Sironar-S, 360 mm f 8 Nikkor-T, and 500mm f 11 Nikkor-T. For detailed close-up work, we borrow from each other a 120mm f 5.6 Schneider Macro Symmar lens. We also frequently use Mamiya 645-1000s medium format cameras for wildlife work and landscape photography. Our Mamiya lenses are 45mm f 2.8 S, 80mm f 2.8, 210mm f 4 C, and 500mm f 5.6. All of the photographs in this book were taken on 4x5-inch and 120mm format Fuji Velvia RVP, Fuji Provia RDPII, and Kodak Ektachrome 100 SW transparency films. We prefer to let natural light work its wonder, so filters were not used to create these images.